In Memory of

Joseph "Jr." Pataskiewcz

by

Walt & Sue Reyer

FOOTBALL HALL OF **FAMERS**

TERRY BRADSHAW

Greg Roza

APR 1 1 2006

the rosen publishing group's
rosen
central

For Mom, with love

Published in 2003 by The Rosen Publishing Group, Inc.
29 East 21st Street, New York, NY 10010

First Edition

Library of Congress Cataloging-in-Publication Data

Roza, Greg.
Terry Bradshaw / Greg Roza.— 1st ed.
p. cm. — (Football hall of famers)
Includes bibliographical references and index.
Summary: Outlines the life and victories of Pittsburgh Steelers football legend Terry Bradshaw.
ISBN 0-8239-3609-0 (lib. bdg.)
1. Bradshaw, Terry—Juvenile literature. 2. Football players—United States—Biography—Juvenile literature. [1. Bradshaw, Terry. 2. Football players.] I. Title. II. Series.
GV939.B68 A38 2003
796.332'092—dc21

2001007020

Manufactured in the United States of America

Contents

Terry Bradshaw overcame a rocky start to his professional football career and emerged as one of the most successful quarterbacks in the history of the National Football League.

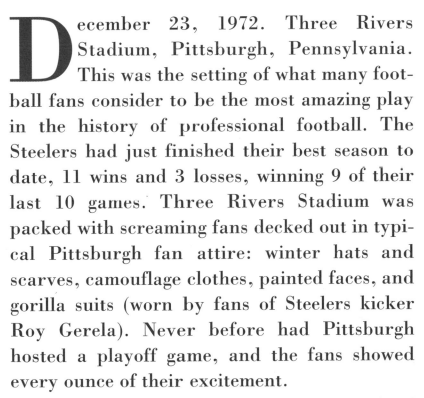

Introduction

Decedemer 23, 1972. Three Rivers Stadium, Pittsburgh, Pennsylvania. This was the setting of what many football fans consider to be the most amazing play in the history of professional football. The Steelers had just finished their best season to date, 11 wins and 3 losses, winning 9 of their last 10 games. Three Rivers Stadium was packed with screaming fans decked out in typical Pittsburgh fan attire: winter hats and scarves, camouflage clothes, painted faces, and gorilla suits (worn by fans of Steelers kicker Roy Gerela). Never before had Pittsburgh hosted a playoff game, and the fans showed every ounce of their excitement.

The Steelers were battling the Oakland Raiders. The rivalry between these two teams would become legendary in the history of professional football, and it may have had its start on this cold, dreary day in Pittsburgh.

Twenty-four-year-old Pittsburgh quarterback Terry Bradshaw had helped lead the Steelers to this game, but he was still fighting to keep his starting position. His stats were decent but not spectacular. His career depended on this game, and he knew it. All his life, he had dreamed of playing in the National Football League (NFL), and that dream had come true. But Three Rivers Stadium was the last place he wanted to be on December 23, 1972. Too much was at stake, more than just his career. Over 50,000 fans were screaming for their first playoff win ever, and Bradshaw had to deliver. Could he get the job done?

And Then the Unthinkable Happened

The game was a long, hard, defensive battle between the silver-and-black Raiders and the black-and-yellow Steelers. The Raiders had stifled Bradshaw's powerful throwing arm all day, but he managed to get the Steelers close enough to the end zone in the second half for two field goals, making the score 6–0 with under four minutes to go in the fourth quarter. With just over a minute left to play in the game, Oakland quarterback Kenny "the Snake" Stabler scrambled past a blitzing Steeler defense and sprinted 30 yards into the end zone, scoring the first touchdown of the game. The extra point kick put Oakland ahead, 7–6. After struggling for 59 minutes, the Steelers were seeing their first playoff win ever slip away. Even the team's owner, Art Rooney, left his seat before the end of the game and went to the locker room to comfort the losing team on a game well played.

Terry Bradshaw also saw their chances dwindling, but he knew he had to play it cool. Bradshaw knew that it was his job to appear confident and in control. He took to the field with a determined stride, despite the fact that his knees were shaking and, deep down, he thought the game was over.

The Amazing Play

With under a minute to play, the Steelers had to cover 80 yards to win the game. Bradshaw's first pass was incomplete. His second was knocked away by Jack Tatum, an Oakland defender who had been a thorn in the side of the Steeler offense all day. Tatum knocked Bradshaw's third pass away as well, and things were looking bleak.

It was fourth down and 10 with 20 seconds to play, and the Steelers were still 80 yards away from the end zone. This could be their last play of the 1972 season. The crowd was screaming so loud that Bradshaw could barely hear his teammates. The Oakland defenders were on him as soon as he got the ball from his center. Growling men in silver and black were clawing at him, grabbing his arm, trying to knock him down. Though Bradshaw could barely see his receivers, he kept fighting. He pushed one defender down and shook another away. Suddenly, he glimpsed number 33—his teammate Frenchy Fuqua—open downfield. Bradshaw sent a bullet downfield just as he was leveled by a crowd of Raiders.

Wincing beneath a pile of players, Bradshaw suddenly heard the crowd go wild. He was sure that time had run out by now, and that everything was riding on his pass to Fuqua. As he struggled to his feet, however, Bradshaw saw something that startled him. Fuqua wasn't crossing into the end zone with the football; instead, it was their teammate Franco Harris. They had won the game 13–7! But what had happened? Before he could find out, fans were flocking onto the field to congratulate Bradshaw on leading the Steelers to their first playoff win ever.

Making History

Bradshaw eventually learned what had happened. As Frenchy Fuqua prepared to catch the ball, he had been tackled hard by Raider Jack Tatum. However, Fuqua (and game officials) insisted that the ball bounced off his hands, then off Tatum. As the ball took a tumble through the air, Franco Harris appeared out of nowhere and scooped it up an instant before it touched the turf. The rest is history. This play, quickly

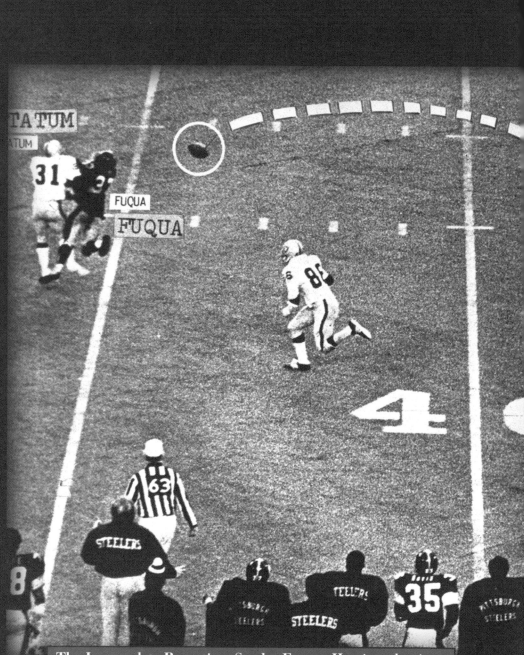

The Immaculate Reception: Steeler Franco Harris rushes in to make a spectacular catch after a pass intended for Frenchy Fuqua was deflected by Jack Tatum of the Oakland Raiders.

dubbed the Immaculate Reception by members of the Pittsburgh sports media, set the stage for the longest and most successful dynasty in the Steelers history: eight straight years in the NFL playoffs, four Super Bowl appearances, and back-to-back Super Bowl victories not once, but twice. Perhaps more important for the Pittsburgh Steelers and their fans, however, this thrilling victory finally signaled an end to their days as a losing team. "The glory days of the Steelers was still two years ahead," Bradshaw once wrote, according to the Web page Bradshaw's Bullet (http://www.mcmillenandwife.com/bradshaw.html), "but we buried our past that day."

Bradshaw hesitates to take credit for the Immaculate Reception. He chalks it up to coincidence and the skill of his teammates, especially Franco Harris. For Bradshaw's fans—and, in truth, for most fans of professional football—it was the play that launched him and the Pittsburgh Steelers into legendary status. Many consider it the single most important and amazing play in the history of football. Whether it was Bradshaw's doing or not, the Immaculate Reception is part of the legend behind the best big-game-winning quarterback the NFL has ever seen.

Even though the Steelers would not make it to the Super Bowl for two more seasons, the playoff game they won against the Oakland Raiders on that December day in 1972 started them on their way to greatness. Regardless of the Immaculate Reception, it was Bradshaw's team spirit, determination, and athletic ability that helped the Steelers win that game. And it's these traits that have helped Bradshaw excel as an athlete and as a human being, from high school to the Hall of Fame and beyond.

All professional athletes dream of making it to the Hall of Fame; it is the greatest honor an athlete can achieve, and only the best of the best make it in. The Immaculate Reception was just the first step for Terry Bradshaw down the demanding but exciting road to the Pro Football Hall of Fame.

Growing Up
on the Farm

Terry Bradshaw was born on September 2, 1948. He grew up in Shreveport, Louisiana, with his father, Bill; his mother, Novis; his elder brother, Gary; and his younger brother, Craig. The Bradshaws led a simple life when Terry was growing up. They were a poor family, but looking back, Terry said that he never noticed their poverty because they had so much fun together.

Almost every summer, Terry and his brothers lived on their grandparents' 40-acre farm in a small town 25 miles south of Shreveport called Hall Summit. This is where the Bradshaw boys learned the value of hard work. They learned how to plow a field and to pick cotton, watermelons, and cantaloupes. The farm had no indoor plumbing, and one of Terry's jobs was cleaning the outhouse. He also learned to drive a team of Clydesdale horses. The work brought Terry and his family very close together. Terry and his brothers also loved to visit their grandparents' farm after school on Fridays.

Bill Bradshaw cared deeply for his family, and he did his best to raise his boys to be good and kind to each other. He had few rules, but the boys were sure to follow them because he was a strict parent. Terry's father knew the importance of education. As Terry and his brothers did their homework every night, Bill did his own homework; he was going to college, studying to become an engineer.

Terry's father liked to take the boys hunting, and Terry loved being in the wilderness with his family. Bill Bradshaw put a lot of effort into teaching his boys to be responsible for themselves, to have respect for others, and to work hard for what they got.

Novis Bradshaw was a devoted mother, and Terry always shared his feelings with her. Just like Bill Bradshaw, Novis taught Terry and his brothers the importance of hard work and good manners. Terry has always been very close to his mother, and he says that he gets his compassion for others from her. She always found it hard to watch him play football and feared that he was going to get hurt. To this day, she still worries about her baby boy.

Religion has always been a great influence in Terry's life. Terry and his brothers were raised as Baptists. Every Sunday, they went to church and listened to a very spirited preacher who kept Terry interested in religion at an early age. Terry even considered becoming a Baptist minister while he was in high school. In addition, Terry has always had a respect for all faiths.

"Stop Bouncing That Football!"

Terry's entire family loved football. Terry's father encouraged his sons to organize games in their backyard whenever they had the time. And when teams were uneven, Terry's mom filled in. Bill Bradshaw even kept extra panes of glass on hand for the broken windows that were just another part of life at the Bradshaw residence.

Terry Bradshaw poses with a football during negotiations with the Pittsburgh Steelers. Joining the team was the realization of a dream he had had since he was a young boy playing in his family's backyard pickup games.

When he wasn't doing chores, doing homework, or going to school, Terry was throwing a football. It had been an obsession of his since the age of four. In his book *Looking Deep*, Terry says that he would sit in his room and bounce the football off the wall until his father yelled, "Terry, stop bouncing that football!" Then he'd bounce it some more.

Terry would frequently play catch for hours at a time with his brothers or with a friend. When his partners decided to call it a day, Terry would throw the ball onto the roof and catch it when it rolled off, or throw the ball through an old tire. He played with his footballs so much that the laces wore out and he would have to repair them with old shoelaces. One day, while punting a football around the backyard, Terry's old worn-out football exploded on the end of his foot!

When Terry was just seven years old, he told his father he was going to play in the NFL when he grew up. Did his father believe him? Maybe not, but Terry always believed it. "And I also believed I would win four Super Bowls and get elected into the Hall of Fame," Terry once wrote in his book *It's Only a Game*, "but I didn't tell him that."

2 School Years

Terry Bradshaw admits today that he was not a very good student when he was young. He had trouble sitting still in class. His mother used to call him a "squirmer." If a subject did not interest him, he didn't even try to understand it. Terry's mother even took him to a few doctors when he was a boy, hoping to find out why he had such a hard time concentrating in school. "Boys will be boys," the doctors said, and so Terry continued to do poorly in school.

Instead of focusing on his classes, Terry put all of his effort into football. Football allowed him to use up all the extra energy he always had. Terry threw a football whenever he could, determined to get better at it. This may help explain why Terry was such a good quarterback, and why he could throw the ball so much farther than other people could.

Choosing a Position

Terry began playing little league football when he was nine years old. At the time, he wasn't a very big kid, and no one felt that he had any special talent. In his first game, he played offensive guard. (The player in this position is responsible for guarding the quarterback.) During this game, Terry tried to tackle a boy who was older and much bigger than he was. As the boy came running at him, Terry closed his eyes and dove at him. He missed the boy completely! Terry discovered that he did not know how to tackle very well and that offensive guard was not the best position for him.

Next, his coach decided to try Terry out in the tailback position. It is the tailback's job to run with the ball after the quarterback hands it to him and try to score points. Sometimes the quarterback may also throw the ball to the tailback. Terry liked this position at first, especially because it gave him the chance to carry the ball and score. He soon lost interest in the tailback position, however, after he was creamed by a defensive player. After that, Terry's coach decided to put him on the bench for a while.

Getting Noticed

At first, Terry had difficulty getting noticed by his coaches. No matter how hard he tried, he failed to land a starting position on a team. Even though he often sat on the bench, Terry continued to practice throwing the football. He even played baseball for a while and was pitcher for his team. When he wasn't throwing a football or a baseball, Terry would throw whatever else he could get his hands on, including "cow chips" from the farm.

When Terry was 13, he and his friends tried out for the junior high school team. Everyone but Terry made it. Terry was convinced that he deserved a place on the team, so he went to practice one day in the hopes that the coach would notice him. He grabbed an extra ball and began throwing it by himself not far from where the coach was directing practice.

By this time, Terry could throw a football about 50 yards! Suddenly, Terry saw the coach running in his direction, and he got scared. He thought he was going to be in trouble. Instead, the coach asked him where he had learned to throw the ball so far. Terry proudly told him that he had been throwing the ball like that since fourth grade. The coach rushed Terry into the locker room and found a uniform for him right away.

By eighth grade, Terry could throw the ball 60 yards. But he didn't make it to starting quarterback until ninth grade.

High School

When he made it to the Woodlawn High School football team in Shreveport, Terry sat on the bench a lot. Football was (and still is) a popular sport in the South, and there were a lot of good players on the team. Their home games often drew crowds of about 15,000 people. Even though he wasn't starting, Terry was happy to be on the team. Sitting on the bench taught him several valuable lessons. He learned to practice hard to make the cut, and he continued to believe in his own ability.

Javelin Star

When Terry was a sophomore in high school, the track coach asked him to throw the javelin after seeing how far he could throw the football. Terry had learned how to throw a javelin by looking at pictures in an encyclopedia. He wasn't really sure about how he was supposed to do it, but he decided to "just chunk it" and see what happened. In his first track meet, Terry threw the javelin 175 feet and won first place in the event. In his junior year, he beat the state champion.

Terry had a big senior year. He started throwing the javelin over 200 feet as he prepared for the state track meet. When it came time to compete, however, Terry surprised everyone, including himself, by throwing the javelin 244 feet, 11¾ inches! This was a new national record. Soon after, reporters came by to interview him, giving him his first real taste of stardom. Terry's experience throwing the

javelin taught him that he could succeed at anything he put his mind to.

Starting Quarterback

That year (1965–1966), Terry also became the
starting quarterback for his high school team. He
had a strong arm and lots of natural talent, but
he still needed experience. His high school football team had a very good season that year. They
were good enough to be in the state finals, but
they lost the game in part because of an interception that Terry threw. Despite the disappointing
end to the season, Terry had performed well
enough to draw the attention of a few colleges.
More colleges offered him track and field scholarships than football scholarships, but he still
made an impression on the gridiron with his ability as a football player.

As Terry's senior year drew to a close, he
received over 200 scholarship offers from colleges all around the country. He even received a
few offers from colleges in Europe. While Terry
was certainly flattered, he turned down every
one of those schools because they were offering

him track scholarships. Terry did not want to throw a javelin; he wanted to throw a football.

The Louisiana Boy Stays Put

Terry played well enough in his senior year to draw the attention of a few big football schools, too, including Florida State University, Texas A & M, Mississippi State, and Notre Dame. The first school to take a serious interest in him was Baylor University in Waco, Texas. Terry considered going to Baylor for several reasons: Baylor had a great football program and it was a Baptist school. When the Baptist recruiters heard that Terry had considered becoming a Baptist minister, they decided to invite him for a visit. Terry was very disappointed with the experience. He thought the school was too "mature" for him. The student he stayed with on the campus was a boy he had known from Shreveport. When the boy offered him alcohol and cigarettes, Terry decided it was not the school for him.

At this point, Terry knew that he wanted to stay in Louisiana. He wanted to be near his friends and family, and he was nervous about

Terry Bradshaw struggled to get playing time on his college team until he became the team's star quarterback in his junior year.

going to a large school. Louisiana State University in Baton Rouge also offered Terry a scholarship. The recruiting staff at LSU made frequent visits to the Bradshaw residence and pressured him to sign on with them. They even picked him up and drove him to Baton Rouge to tour the campus. They constantly told Terry that LSU was the perfect place for him because they had a tradition of recruiting talented quarterbacks. They also suggested that he would never make it to the pros unless he enrolled in a "big-time" football school like LSU.

Eventually, Terry gave in, but he still wasn't sure it was the right school for him. LSU had a well-known football program, and Terry was nervous about going to a school where he would have to compete with such little playing experience (he had completed only one full year of football in high school). As confident as he was in his own abilities, Terry was shy around other people, especially in an environment where the competition was much harder than anything he was used to. Terry was so unsure about going to LSU that he purposely failed the entrance exam—twice. While at the time he was relieved, it was a decision that would later come back to haunt him.

Terry eventually decided to attend a smaller school that was closer to his hometown: Louisiana Tech in Ruston, Louisiana. The scouts from Louisiana Tech were overjoyed to hear that someone as talented as Terry wanted to attend their college and play football for them. Terry's brother, Gary, was already studying at Louisiana Tech, as were several of his friends, so it seemed like a good choice.

On the Bench Again

At Louisiana Tech, Terry was once again waiting in the wings behind another talented quarterback named Phil Robertson. After a whole year without seeing any action, Terry contacted coaches at Florida State University—another school that had expressed interest in him—to see if they would like to sign him up. They were quick to accept.

When Terry arrived at FSU during the summer between his freshman and sophomore years, the coaching staff harshly told him to turn around and go home. The coaching staff from Louisiana Tech had found out about Terry's plans and had threatened to charge the FSU coaches with tampering. Disappointed, Terry returned to Ruston afraid that he would have to sit on the bench for another year.

Terry's sophomore year was like a roller-coaster ride. The starting quarterback, Phil Robertson, quit the team before the season started, and Terry thought that he would finally be the starter. However, the coaching staff at Louisiana Tech were not being honest with Terry. They secretly begged Robertson to return to the team while at the same time promising Terry the starting position. As they boarded the bus for their first game that season, Phil Robertson got on with them. Terry found out minutes before the game that the coaches had begged Phil to come back. Terry was so mad, he threw the ball at the coach on the sidelines before the game.

However, Phil was injured in the first minutes of the game, and Terry came in to throw for

250 yards, leading Louisiana Tech to a big win. The quarterback job bounced back and forth between Terry and Phil all season, causing both quarterbacks to grow more and more angry with the coaching staff. At the end of that year, Phil Robertson quit the team for good, leaving the starting position to Terry for his junior year.

Terry's Big Break

Terry realized that if he really wanted to make it to the pros, he needed to step up and play as well as he knew he could. Terry worked very hard, training more than ever before. He used to wait until late at night and sneak into the campus stadium, where he would turn on the lights and practice throwing. When the campus police kicked him out of the stadium, he practiced in the school gymnasium.

Hard Work Pays Off

Terry's junior year was a turning point in his career. Due to his determination and dedication to practicing, he exploded onto the college football scene and people began to recognize him. He led the nation in total offensive yardage that year, setting the stage for his senior year, which was even better. Most quarterbacks looked to the sidelines between downs for guidance from the coaches. However, Terry's coaches in college encouraged him to call his own plays based on what he thought would work best. (Of course, this happened after they realized that he liked to improvise during games; Terry played his best when he was allowed to see what the defense was going to do and then beat them to the punch.) This allowed him to gain more confidence on the field. During the 1969 season, Terry helped the team win 9 games out of 11, and he led them to the NCAA College Division Mideast Championship.

ABC broadcast the championship game to the whole country. It was Terry's first televised game. Everyone he knew was watching, and the stands were packed with pro scouts. Terry threw three touchdown passes and ran for two touchdowns. After the game, he was presented with the MVP (most valuable player) trophy. Terry

This display at Louisiana Tech celebrates Terry's impressive career as the college's star quarterback from 1968 to 1970.

was selected to play in the Senior Bowl that year. This was an exhibition game in which the most talented seniors in the country participated. Once again Terry was selected MVP. Terry's coaches had been shocked to see Terry excel so quickly after such a slow start. Terry, however, had known all along what he was capable of. The MVP trophies were great accomplishments, but Terry was most excited about impressing dozens of NFL scouts.

Record Breaker Bradshaw

During the 1969 season, Terry had broken all the passing and total offense records at Louisiana Tech. And he still holds those records to this day. Soon, pro team scouts were calling his house wanting to speak with the young football star. Terry's father insisted on being his manager, and Terry was glad to have him in that role. Bill was an honest, hardworking man, but he lacked the business knowledge necessary to get Terry the best deal possible. The Baltimore Colts' legendary head coach, Don Shula, unexpectedly called the Bradshaw residence one day and told Bill Bradshaw that he'd trade six players for Terry. But Bill refused to listen to any offers because he wanted to do things by the book. Rumor had it that Terry would be picked first in the approaching football draft, something that had never happened to a player from a small-town school like Louisiana Tech. Terry's dream of playing in the NFL was becoming a reality.

Drafted!

After stunning the college football world during his junior and senior years, Terry and his father were sure he would be selected in the upcoming NFL entry draft. They figured he would be taken in the third or fourth round, but they had another surprise coming.

As the 1970 NFL entry draft approached, Terry began receiving calls from pro teams expressing their desire to take him in the first round. The two main contenders were the worst teams of the 1969 season: the Chicago Bears of the NFC (National Football Conference) Central Division, and the Pittsburgh Steelers of the AFC

ROUND #1

1 PITT - BRADSHAW, Te
2 GB - McCOY, MIKE
3 CLE - PHIPPS, M
4 BOS - OLSEN
5 BUF - COWLIN
6 PHI - ZABEL
7 CINN - R D, M
8 ST. L - S NT,
9 S. FRAN -
10 N. OK -
11 DEN -
12 ATL -
13 NYG -

The Pittsburgh Steelers' owner, Art Rooney, *(left)* gestures as he discusses the signing of quarterback Terry Bradshaw on January 27, 1970. Rooney's son, Dan, looks on.

President Richard Nixon measures his hand against Terry Bradshaw's during Bradshaw's visit to the White House on March 7, 1970.

(American Football Conference) Central Division. Both teams finished the season with only one win. A coin was tossed to determine who would get to draft the hottest college quarterback.

Early the next day, the Bradshaw family discovered that the Steelers had won the coin toss. They had taken Terry as the first selection in the 1970 NFL entry draft. Shortly after they heard the good news, Dan Rooney, son of the Steelers' owner Art Rooney, called Terry to welcome him to the team. Chuck Noll, the coach of the Steelers, also called to congratulate him.

Reporters soon began showing up, eager to interview the first-round draft pick.

Terry was asked to come to Pittsburgh to participate in a news conference. It was his first time in Pittsburgh and in the North. It was a whole new experience for him, and although he was nervous, he loved every minute of it. Fans crowded around him during the news conference. Camera lights flashed, and reporters asked him questions. Terry smiled a big smile and gladly answered all their questions with confidence.

Before Terry even got to training camp, his picture was on the cover of *Sports Illustrated* and *Newsweek*. But Terry had no time to think about his newfound fame. He was moving to a place far away from his home, his family, and his friends. Pittsburgh was very different from Shreveport, and he needed to get used to his new surroundings quickly. The 1970 NFL season was just around the corner.

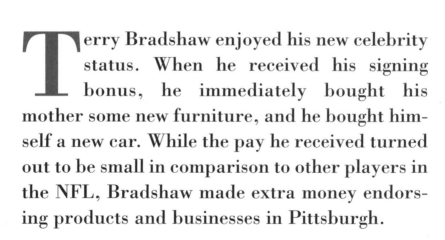

Turning Pro

Terry Bradshaw enjoyed his new celebrity status. When he received his signing bonus, he immediately bought his mother some new furniture, and he bought himself a new car. While the pay he received turned out to be small in comparison to other players in the NFL, Bradshaw made extra money endorsing products and businesses in Pittsburgh.

City Living

It took some time for young Bradshaw to grow accustomed to his new surroundings. Bradshaw admits today that he was somewhat naive when he was drafted into the NFL. For a farm boy from the South living in a northern city, things could not have been more different. People recognized him when he went places, which was very strange for him at first. Bradshaw was particularly shy around women. While he had dated a few girls in high school and college, he had never had a serious girlfriend. As soon as he got drafted, however, he received a large number of letters from women who wanted to meet him.

Another eye-opening experience for Bradshaw was meeting and playing football with African Americans. Shreveport had been a segregated community when Bradshaw was growing up, and he had known very few black people. Because of this, in his early days with the Steelers, Bradshaw actually made the terrible mistake of referring to his black teammates as "colored" people. This lapse didn't go unchecked for long, however, thanks to one of his black teammates—Jon Staggers—who corrected him and taught Bradshaw about African American culture. Bradshaw certainly had not meant to offend anyone, he just didn't know any better. After spending some time with the team, Bradshaw was disappointed to find that although the black players and white players got along on the field, not all of them got along off the field. This is something he was glad to see change more and more the longer he was in the NFL.

Rude Awakening

The Pittsburgh Steelers had never won a playoff game in their 37 years as an NFL team. The Steelers and the town of Pittsburgh were expecting a miracle, and Terry Bradshaw had a lot of big expectations to live up to. Bradshaw soon realized, however, that saving the Steelers would be more difficult than he and everyone else thought. Before Bradshaw could save the team, he had to get used to playing football in the pros, and that wasn't an easy task.

There were many noticeable differences between college football and pro football. The biggest difference was that pro defensive players hit harder—a lot harder. Bradshaw also realized that he wasn't going to be able to run with the ball when he couldn't find a receiver like he did in college. Every time he tried to he got clobbered by a pack of defensive players. The high level of play unnerved Bradshaw right from the start, and it took him a while to get used to it. But there were other differences as well. The Steeler coaches—especially head coach Chuck Noll—were much more strict and more demanding than his coaches in high school and college had been. There was no way they were going to let Bradshaw call his own plays, and he had to get used to accepting the plays called by his coaches.

The opinions of Steeler fans were divided on Bradshaw. Many people liked him because they thought he would turn the Steelers into a winning team right away. They called him things like the "Blonde Bomber" and "Terrific Terry." Other Steeler fans thought that the team had wasted their first-round draft pick on a quarterback who hadn't been truly tested in college.

The second group seemed to be correct when the season started and the Steelers still did not play much better than they had during the previous season. On top of this, people soon heard that Bradshaw had failed his entrance exams to LSU. Fans and members of the media in Pittsburgh started calling Bradshaw names like "dummy" and "bumpkin." Even Coach

Steelers head coach Chuck Noll *(left)* was mercilessly critical of his quarterback's football savvy during Bradshaw's early years with Pittsburgh.

Noll called him a dummy during games when he made a bad play. This name stuck with Bradshaw for a long time, and it always made him mad. He wasn't used to people being mean to him. In time, however, he would learn to deal with the negative image people had of him, but as a rookie, it hurt his feelings so much that he nearly quit playing professional football.

A Rough Rookie Season

The 1970 preseason went rather well for the Steelers. They won four out of five games. Bradshaw shared the quarterback position with a player named Terry Hanratty. Even though Bradshaw was told he would have the starting position once the season began, he knew he had to compete against another quarterback to be a first-string player.

Bradshaw started his first game as a pro against the Houston Oilers. He was hit so hard he found it difficult to concentrate on making passes. He threw an interception and was sacked twice. Halfway through the game he was booed. Coach Noll decided to pull him out of the game and put in Hanratty instead. Bradshaw felt as if he had let everyone down, and he didn't like feeling that way. The fans, the coaches, and the players had all been counting on him. This was one of Bradshaw's worst moments.

That first loss taught Bradshaw a lot. Professional football sure was different from college ball. In college, if Bradshaw couldn't find someone to throw the ball to he would run with it himself. Also, in college ball, Bradshaw was usually bigger than most of the players, and it had always been easy to break tackles. In the pros, many of the players were bigger than he was, and they hit much harder than college defenders did. Bradshaw soon learned the importance of looking for and finding secondary receivers to throw to.

The season continued to be difficult. In some games, Bradshaw would do just OK, but in most games he did terribly. He suddenly felt like no one trusted him to lead the team. And he was right.

Meanwhile, his reputation in Pittsburgh continued to get worse. Fans booed him wherever he went; they even booed his mom

During his rookie season, Bradshaw often found it difficult to run the football when he could not find an open receiver.

when she came to visit him. He received nasty letters, and reporters and sports announcers made fun of him. In his book *It's Only a Game*, Terry remembers when legendary sportscaster Howard Cosell called him "the number one flop in the National Football League" during an interview. Coach Noll continued to scold him for playing poorly. Things got so bad that, at one point, Bradshaw told a reporter that he was considering quitting football and becoming a minister. Once again people used this as a reason to make fun of him, calling him "crybaby."

In the final game of the season, against the Philadelphia Eagles, Bradshaw was required to play the punter's position while Hanratty started at quarterback. This was the ultimate slap in the face for Bradshaw, and it didn't help that he was not a very good punter. The season ended, and the Steelers did not make it to the playoffs. Bradshaw threw only 6 touchdown passes all year; he threw 24 interceptions. And the Pittsburgh fans continued to show their dislike for Bradshaw.

Bradshaw Gains Confidence

When the 1970 season ended, Bradshaw felt horrible about letting his team down. Just as in high school and college, he knew he had to try harder. In the off-season, Bradshaw practiced extra hard. He threw the ball to anyone who would catch it, and when he was alone, he'd practice by himself. He had something to prove to the Steelers, to the Steelers' fans, to his fans back home, and, most of all, to himself.

At the beginning of the 1971 season, Bradshaw was surprised to find that he was still the number-one quarterback. His hard work and determination began to pay off that year. A new assistant coach named Babe Parilli gave him a lot of advice. Parilli explained things to Bradshaw, and through him Bradshaw developed a better perspective on professional football. Bradshaw also concentrated harder on the Steelers' playbook, as well as his options on the field.

The Steelers won only six games in 1971, but Bradshaw had doubled the number of completed passes and the number of touchdown passes he had made during the 1970 season.

Even though he still hadn't completely won over the Steelers' fans, he was improving.

Building a Winning Team

The next year was even better for the Steelers. The roster was starting to become one that would carry the team to greatness. Bradshaw had many talented and devoted teammates, but a handful of them stood out from the crowd. "Mean" Joe Greene was a tall, powerful, and aggressive defensive tackle who always looked out for his teammates; it was scary to be on the other side of the line from him. Jack Lambert was a tough but quiet middle linebacker who usually kept to himself but helped to lead the team both in the locker room and on the field. Cornerback Mel Blount was just as tough but not as quiet. These three players helped lead a defense that soon came to be known as the Steel Curtain because of their ability to stop other teams from scoring.

On offense, Bradshaw was lucky to have two of the best wide receivers football has ever seen: Lynn Swann and John Stallworth.

"Mean" Joe Greene struts his stuff in this 1979 Coca-Cola commercial that plays on his tough-guy image. Greene shows kindness to an awestruck young fan who offers him a Coke.

Bradshaw often had trouble deciding which of these players to throw to. In 1972, the Steelers drafted a running back named Franco Harris. Harris was a quiet player, but he was also tough and intelligent. In the huddle, if Harris told Bradshaw to get him the ball, Bradshaw got him the ball, and Harris did great things with it.

In 1972, these determined athletes worked to give the Steelers their best season yet. They won 11 games that year. Once again, all eyes were on Terry Bradshaw. Interest in the young quarterback reached a whole new level when he led the team to their first playoff win in Steeler history, ending in perhaps the most spectacular and contested play of all time: the Immaculate Reception. The 1972 season ended with a 17–21 loss to the Miami Dolphins, but the team had tasted victory, and they wanted more.

Getting Better All the Time

The Steelers made it to the playoffs in 1973, only to be defeated in the first round by the Oakland Raiders. Although Terry was beginning to win over some fans, many others—and the Pittsburgh media—were still very tough on him. They had expected a Super Bowl from this young college star, and when it had not happened right away, they became very mean. The longer it took Bradshaw to reach the Super Bowl, the meaner some of them became.

As Bradshaw matured as a professional football player, he gained confidence in his own ability and stopped letting public opinion bother him. Instead, he concentrated on his game. Bradshaw also realized that those who thought of him as a dummy—thereby underestimating his abilities—were often caught off guard by his skills on the field. Another thing that helped Bradshaw was that he started calling his own plays again. Although Coach Noll would send him out onto the field with a play, Bradshaw would surprise him by doing something completely different. He didn't care that it made Coach Noll mad. He felt he knew what was best for his offense.

Bradshaw also learned to read the defense, something he had not done very well at first. He could look at the defense just before a play and get a good idea of what they were going to do. This not only made his job easier, it also made him a much better quarterback.

A New Frame of Mind

In 1974, Bradshaw was once again benched. But this time it wasn't because there was someone better ahead of him. The professional players went on strike in 1974, and many starters sat on the bench while owners and players worked things out. The time Bradshaw spent on the bench caused him to rethink his career. While he certainly had improved over the past few years, he still wasn't perfectly happy. He felt as if he had given up on his dream, and he was angry with himself for that. He was playing in the NFL, but he still needed to win a Super Bowl.

Bradshaw decided to relax and start thinking more positively. It occurred to him that the best way to get to the Super Bowl was to go back to the basics of football. He started to develop a simple but efficient style of football. Nothing fancy, just quick and powerful.

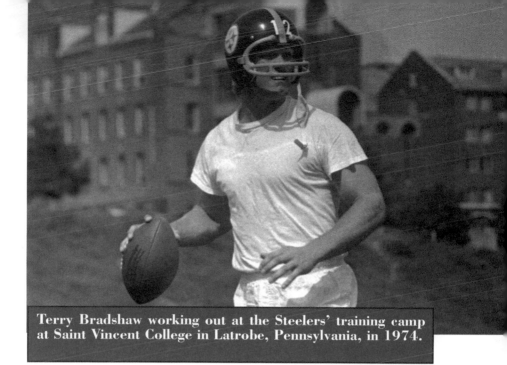

Terry Bradshaw working out at the Steelers' training camp at Saint Vincent College in Latrobe, Pennsylvania, in 1974.

Bradshaw had always hated throwing short passes. To him, they were too easy. He preferred to throw long passes, at least 15 yards, but often 50 and 60 yards. He loved to thrill the crowd and get them cheering for more. With Lynn Swann and John Stallworth to throw to, the Steelers' passing game quickly became a serious threat to the other teams. Since it was so reliable, the Steelers began working on a strong running game. This was easy with a player like Franco Harris on the team. They would run the ball most of the time, moving it slowly but surely down the field. Then, suddenly, Bradshaw would drop back and throw a long pass. Most of the time he hit his receivers perfectly, often for points. If Bradshaw knew his opponents were expecting a short pass or a quick run, he would surprise them by dropping back and throwing a long pass. This made it more difficult to defend against the Steelers' offense.

Many of the things Bradshaw did were out of the ordinary. Few quarterbacks call their own plays, and that alone made him unique in the NFL. Something else that made him stand out was that he asked his teammates what they thought they should do while they were in the huddle. "How's it look?" he would say in the huddle, and wait for some good advice from his running backs, wide receivers, and even his linemen. Thanks to all these elements, the Steelers soon became one of the best teams in the NFL.

A Rising Star

Once the football strike of 1974 was over, the Steelers got back to work. That year was to be the first of six consecutive years in which the Steelers would be the best team in the AFC Central Division. They defeated the Buffalo Bills in the first game of the playoffs, 32–14. Although much of the credit for winning this game needs to be given to Franco Harris and Lynn Swann, Terry Bradshaw stole the show. He threw for 209 yards that day, and he ran for 48 yards. Bradshaw led the Steelers to four touchdowns in the second quarter, setting an NFL playoff record.

As usual, the Steelers had to make it past the Oakland Raiders to become champions of the AFC. The winner would go on to play the NFC champion in Super Bowl IX. Having to overcome the Raiders in the playoffs had become a customary event for the Steelers. Bradshaw was coming off one of his best games ever and felt up to the challenge. He was relaxed and ready to play.

Pittsburgh won the game, 24–13. Bradshaw led the team to three fourth-quarter touchdowns to win the game. He was overjoyed to help the Pittsburgh Steelers reach their first Super Bowl in 42 years. However, Bradshaw's joy was slightly overshadowed by the media's persistent jibes. In the week before Super Bowl IX, many reporters asked Bradshaw questions about his intelligence; one writer even asked him what his IQ was. It became apparent to Bradshaw that these were questions he would have to deal with for the rest of his career, no matter what he did on or off the field. He was going to have to learn to be thick-skinned.

Super Bowl IX

The Pittsburgh Steelers were playing the NFC champs, the Minnesota Vikings. This was the Vikings' third Super Bowl appearance in six

Pittsburgh Steelers quarterback Terry Bradshaw (number 12) calls out a play on the line during Super Bowl IX against the Minnesota Vikings at Tulane Stadium in New Orleans, Louisiana, on January 12, 1975.

Terry Bradshaw makes an 11-yard rush for a first down during Super Bowl IX.

years. They were led by a great quarterback, Fran Tarkenton. Tarkenton was a smart, popular player, and most reporters wanted to know how someone like Bradshaw could hope to beat him. Many thought he was too stupid to beat someone like Fran Tarkenton and his Minnesota Vikings.

The stands of Tulane Stadium in New Orleans, Louisiana, were filled with over 80,000 people, and every one of them was screaming. This was before the game had even started. Music blared, camera flashes popped, and fireworks exploded. Bradshaw was awed by the sights and sounds around him. There were reporters and camera crews everywhere. He had never seen anything like it. He remained nervous for most of the game.

A Defensive Battle

The defenses for both teams—the Steel Curtain and the Purple People Eaters—were in rare form. (The Vikings' colors are purple and yellow.) It was a close game, and neither quarterback could throw a touchdown pass for most of the game. The best player early in the game was Franco Harris, the only player to score a touchdown.

Late in the fourth quarter, the Steelers were winning 9–6. Suddenly, Bradshaw felt a great sense of confidence. He needed to prove to all those reporters and fans that he was smart enough to beat the great Fran Tarkenton. Players on both sides of the ball could sense Bradshaw's resolve as he marched the Steelers down the field. Every camera in the stadium was focused on him. The Vikings did what they could to stop the advancing Steeler offense, but it was too late. Bradshaw threw the only touchdown pass of the game with only three minutes left to play. The Steelers won the game, 16–6!

Bradshaw certainly was proud of his contribution to Super Bowl IX. Looking back on the entire season, however, he felt that his contribution had been small compared to that of other players. The Steeler defense really saved the day by shutting down the Vikings' offense. Franco Harris scored a touchdown and won the MVP award for setting a Super Bowl record, 158 yards in 34 carries. As happy as Bradshaw was with seeing his dream come true, he still felt like there was something left to do—win another Super Bowl.

Super Bowl X

The Steelers finished the 1975 season with 12 wins and 2 losses. Bradshaw started in every game that season, and his statistics were much better than those for the 1974 season. The Steelers defeated the Baltimore Colts in the first round of the playoffs, then beat the Oakland Raiders in the second round. They were going back to the Super Bowl.

Steelers quarterback Terry Bradshaw yells out signals before taking the snap from center Mike Webster during an NFL playoff game against the Baltimore Colts.

This time they were battling the Dallas Cowboys. The Cowboys had a superstar quarterback, Roger Staubach. Bradshaw himself was particularly nervous about the Cowboys' defense, which was nearly unbeatable.

The Cowboys were trash talkers, and they openly laughed at the Pittsburgh Steelers. Steeler receiver Lynn Swann was recovering from a concussion he had suffered in the last game against the Raiders, and there was a chance that he wouldn't make it to the Super Bowl. When one member of the Cowboys suggested to the media that he was afraid to play, Swann rose to the challenge. The Steelers weren't going to be intimidated by any team.

Bradshaw Silences the Cowboys

Staubach started the game with a touchdown pass to one of his receivers, and Bradshaw responded right away with another touchdown pass. As the game progressed, Swann proved that he was not afraid of the Dallas Cowboys. He was clearly the best player on the field that day. He caught four passes for 161 yards, setting a Super Bowl record. This included a stunning 64-yard pass from Bradshaw that won the game. With just three minutes left in the game, the Steelers were winning 15–10. Bradshaw dropped back to pass, looking for Swann. As he let the ball go, he knew it was the best pass he had ever thrown, even though he never saw Swann catch it. Seconds after throwing the ball, Bradshaw was hit in the jaw by Dallas defenseman Larry Cole and knocked unconscious. He had to be carried from the field.

When Bradshaw came to in the locker room, his smiling father filled him in on what had happened. He had completed the pass to Swann, who had run the last five yards into the end zone to score the game-winning touchdown. With less than three minutes left to play, the Dallas quarterback scored another touchdown to make the score 21–14. Everyone held their breath as Staubach nearly scored yet another touchdown, but instead he threw an interception in the last seconds of the game. The Steelers had won their second Super Bowl in a row.

Lynn Swann makes a diving pass reception during Super Bowl X at the Orange Bowl in Miami, Florida, on January 18, 1976.

The only player to outshine Bradshaw that day was Lynn Swann, who won the MVP award. Bradshaw had a better game than the previous Super Bowl, throwing for 209 yards and two touchdowns. He also avoided throwing interceptions. It was this game that officially made Bradshaw one of the best big-game winning quarterbacks of all time. However, the best was yet to come.

Super Bowl XIII

Even though the Steelers were the AFC Central Division champs for the next two seasons, they did not make it to Super Bowl XI or Super Bowl XII. Nonetheless, they were always in the running, and many teams considered them the team to beat. This was because they had so many superstars on their team and because they were a really motivated bunch.

The 1978 season was the best year of Bradshaw's career. He led the Steelers to 14 wins that season, and they rarely scored less than 20 points in a game. He threw for 2,915 yards in the regular season, and scored 28 touchdowns—the most touchdowns of any quarterback that season. He was elected to the All-Pro Team for the second time and was declared 1978 NFL Player of the Year. He also won his second consecutive Steelers MVP award.

Once again, the Steelers were face-to-face with the Cowboys. The Cowboys were still the trash talkers they had always been, especially after winning the last Super Bowl. As told in *It's Only a Game*, when asked about the Super Bowl matchup, a player for the Cowboys named Thomas "Hollywood" Henderson told reporters, "Bradshaw couldn't spell 'cat' if you spotted him the 'c' and the 't.' "

Bradshaw laughed the comment off in front of the cameras. He even made a few jokes about it himself: "It's 'o,' isn't it?" The verbal exchange instantly became famous. Terry Bradshaw and Thomas Henderson even appeared on the cover of *Newsweek* the week before the game. What Bradshaw didn't tell people was that he considered the comment mean and nasty. It was just one more reason for him to go out and win big.

Go Ask Henderson If I'm Dumb Today

Super Bowl XIII turned out to be one of the most exciting Super Bowls ever played. The score was close for most of the game. Bradshaw injured his shoulder in the first half, and everyone on the Steelers was very worried. Everyone except for Bradshaw, that is. Bradshaw later wrote, in his book *Looking Deep*, "Even though over the next few years I played better, this was the only game in which I knew I was in total control of everything that happened on the field. It was eerie."

After two consecutive touchdown passes, Bradshaw had the Steelers ahead of the Cowboys 35–17 with less than 10 minutes to play. Many of the players were already celebrating on the sidelines. This made Bradshaw mad because he knew what Roger Staubach could do. After all, Staubach had almost led his Cowboys to a last-minute victory over the Steelers in Super Bowl X. And that almost happened again in Super Bowl XIII; Staubach rallied the Cowboys to two more touchdowns, making the score 35–31. That was how the game would end.

Bradshaw set new Super Bowl records by scoring four touchdowns and throwing for 318 yards. He averaged about 10 yards per pass. He was unanimously selected MVP of Super Bowl XIII. According to SportingNews.com, after the game, as reporters crowded around Bradshaw for interviews, he proudly remarked, "Go and ask Henderson if I was dumb today."

Super Bowl XIV

During the 1979 season, Bradshaw threw for 3,724 yards, the most of his career. Remarkably enough, the Steelers were headed back to the Super Bowl for a fourth time. If they were victorious, they would be the only team to ever win back-to-back Super Bowls twice, a monumental task. "It seemed like there was always another carrot out there to chase," Bradshaw wrote in his book *Looking Deep*.

Making History

The Steelers met the Los Angeles Rams in Super Bowl XIV. While the Steelers were the favorite, Bradshaw knew it would be a hard

Terry Bradshaw prepares to make a pass during Super Bowl XIII, which the Steelers played against the Dallas Cowboys on January 21, 1979.

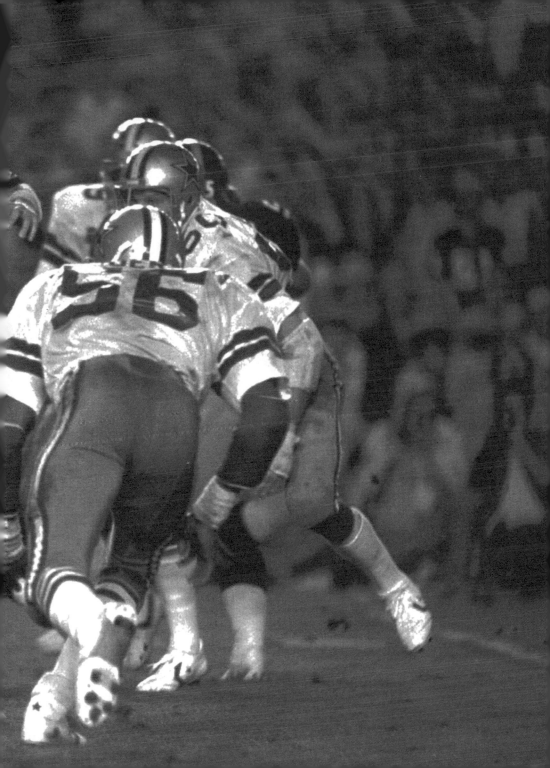

game. Their defense wasn't as powerful as it had once been, and Bradshaw knew it would be up to him and the offense to win the game. The score was close for most of the game, but the Rams kept finding ways to stay a step ahead of them. By the fourth quarter, the Rams were winning by two points, 19–17. Bradshaw knew it was time to turn up the heat.

With time quickly ticking away in the fourth quarter, Coach Noll decided they needed to throw a long pass to beat the Rams' defense. Bradshaw had practiced a special passing play with John Stallworth eight times in the week before the Super Bowl, but they couldn't make it work. Bradshaw and Stallworth were nervous about trying the play, but Coach Noll insisted.

It was third down and eight. Bradshaw got the ball from the center and backed up to pass, waiting just long enough for Stallworth to sprint down the field. Bradshaw let the pass go, and it sailed just over the reach of the defender who was covering Stallworth. The ball landed perfectly in Stallworth's hands, and without breaking stride, Stallworth ran the rest of the

Terry Bradshaw hugs his wife, JoJo Starbuck, after leading the Pittsburgh Steelers to victory in Super Bowl XIII.

way into the end zone. The Steelers pulled ahead with this 73-yard pass, 24–19!

With about five minutes to play, the Rams moved quickly down the field. It looked like they were going to score, but Jack Lambert of the Steelers intercepted a pass from Rams quarterback Vince Ferragamo. Soon it was third down and seven yards to go, and the Steelers were still deep in their own territory. Coach Noll called the same special play again. Bradshaw threw another perfect pass to John Stallworth, who again made an amazing catch. "One of the great catches in Super Bowl history," Bradshaw wrote in *Looking Deep*. A few plays later, Franco Harris ran in for the final touchdown of the game, making the score 31–19. The Steelers had won an unprecedented fourth Super Bowl.

Terry Bradshaw won his second consecutive Super Bowl MVP award by throwing for 309 yards and two touchdowns. Bradshaw also set several Super Bowl records, including most passing yards and most touchdowns. He and the Steelers had accomplished the impossible.

Terry Bradshaw raises his arms in celebration after winning Super Bowl XIV. He was named the game's most valuable player.

The amazing accomplishments of the Pittsburgh Steelers would ensure that many of them would make it into the Pro Football Hall of Fame. After four Super Bowl wins and two well-deserved Super Bowl MVP awards, Terry Bradshaw was certain to be one of those inductees. But few people mentioned the Hall of Fame at that point because no one knew what Bradshaw would do next.

Life After the Super Bowl

5

In the years following Super Bowl XIV, the Steelers began to lose their edge. The 1980 season was the first time in eight years that they did not make it into the playoffs. Football fans knew it was the end of the Steeler dynasty. Strangely enough, Bradshaw called the few years after they won Super Bowl XIV his happiest days as a football quarterback. He was playing for a team that truly needed him as a leader. Football seemed more fun to him once the team wasn't under so much pressure to win all the time.

No one could deny that Bradshaw was one of the greatest quarterbacks of all time. Even though some fans and members of the media still considered him to be unintelligent, these comments no longer bothered Terry Bradshaw. Regardless of how reporters felt about him,

Quarterback Terry Bradshaw throws the football before being tackled by a San Diego Chargers defensive player during a game in 1981. Bradshaw's team did not do well that year.

most were eager to interview him because of his colorful speech and the humorous comments he usually made. And, of course, Bradshaw never shied away from the camera.

The End of a Football Career

The list of injuries that Bradshaw sustained over his 14 years as a quarterback is amazing: concussions, broken collarbones, broken ribs, broken fingers, a broken wrist, a broken nose, neck injuries, knee injuries, and torn muscles. Like many football players, Bradshaw had learned to play with injuries and pain. During one season, he even played with a cast on his wrist. In 1982, however, Bradshaw injured the elbow of his throwing arm during practice. This made passing so painful that he resorted to painkilling drugs and shots, something he had never done before.

Bradshaw was only 34 and he felt he could still play football. Because of this, he sat out most of the 1983 season after having surgery on his elbow—he was hoping to wait out the injury instead of retiring. His coaches, teammates, and fans eagerly awaited his return. He was confident that he would be able to put his uniform back on and help his team.

One Last Chance

Bradshaw got the chance to do just that in the second to last game of the 1983 season. His arm felt great, and he started throwing harder and harder in practice. However, a few days before the game, he reinjured the elbow. Though the pain was terrible and he could barely throw the ball, he kept it a secret because he didn't want to let down his team, his coach, and his fans.

When Bradshaw started in his first game of the season against the New York Jets, he seemed just like his old self—he scored two touchdowns by the end of the first quarter. However, by this time, the pain was unbearable and Bradshaw knew he could not go on. He left the field holding his elbow. His last play as a professional football player was a touchdown throw.

Life After Pittsburgh

After the 1983 season, Bradshaw hoped to return to the game after more surgery. But his arm just wouldn't heal properly, and he realized that he would have to retire before the season began in 1984. Bradshaw was heartbroken. He had been playing football for 25 years, and now he would have to leave it all behind.

Terry Bradshaw wasn't the kind of person to sit around and feel sorry for himself. He knew he could find something else he liked to do. He was an animal lover and had always enjoyed the wilderness. He had tried his hand at cattle ranching while playing for the Steelers but had not done so well. He had also tried raising carrier pigeons. Neither of these activities developed into careers for Bradshaw. Since retiring, however, Bradshaw has started a successful horse-breeding farm in Texas.

Bradshaw had developed several talents earlier in his life other than football. Around 1976, he met actor Burt Reynolds. Bradshaw and Reynolds became good friends. Reynolds often asked Bradshaw to play small roles in his movies, including *Hooper*, *Smokey and the Bandit*, and *Cannonball Run*. Bradshaw usually played seemingly dim-witted Southern boys, but he didn't mind. In fact, he had started to enjoy being known as a funny country bumpkin. At the same time that he was acting in movies, Bradshaw began a singing career. Over the years, he has recorded several country-western and gospel albums, and his version of the song "I'm So Lonesome I Could Cry" was in the top ten on the *Billboard* charts.

After spending 14 years in front of the camera on the field, Bradshaw realized that he could build a successful career as a television announcer. Several television networks had already been offering him permanent positions since the 1982 season. Bradshaw was perfect for this type of job—after all, he loved football and he loved to talk.

Learning a New Trade

Bradshaw's first job as an announcer for CBS was just as eye-opening as his first job as a professional quarterback. Despite being one of the best quarterbacks ever to play the game, Bradshaw discovered that he needed to know more about the actual rules of football. Earlier,

The former Pittsburgh Steelers quarterback poses with the album that included his country and western hit song, "I'm So Lonesome I Could Cry."

he had just gone onto the field and played the best game he could, but he had never taken the time to learn all the rules.

Bradshaw also found it difficult to concentrate on learning how to be an announcer. He was still a squirmer. Even today, Bradshaw finds it difficult to sit still for very long. During his career, he saw dozens of doctors due to the numerous injuries he experienced. After he retired from football, however, he decided to once again see some doctors. He was informed that he had attention deficit disorder, or ADD.

CBS's football announcer Terry Bradshaw chats with his partner Vern Lundquist during a broadcast of an NFL game.

ADD makes learning harder for some people because they have trouble focusing on a single task or subject for very long. People with ADD are distracted very easily. Finally knowing why he had such a hard time concentrating was a relief to Bradshaw, but it didn't make announcing games any easier.

Bradshaw's announcing partner, veteran Vern Lundquist, gave him lots of advice and encouragement. Bradshaw has called Lundquist a mentor, and he probably would not have been successful without the elder announcer's help.

Despite the problems, Bradshaw had fun because he just acted like himself. He cracked jokes, he laughed, and he talked about simple things: running, passing, blocking, and tackling.

Bradshaw worked hard to overcome the obstacles in his way. For instance, it wasn't until he watched a game from the announcer's booth that he realized he needed glasses. He had played for 14 years and never once thought about getting glasses. Now he needed to see players and their names and numbers from far away. Another problem he had to overcome was his tendency to talk too much. Sometimes he would talk about Louisiana, his family, his childhood, and other unrelated topics while announcing. On one occasion, Bradshaw was announcing a game on television with Vern Lundquist, and he thought he was doing a fantastic job. A security guard unexpectedly handed Bradshaw a telegram from a viewer who was watching the game. The short and angry message, which can't be repeated here, essentially told him to shut up. Bradshaw began to realize that talking too much could upset some viewers.

Terry Bradshaw *(center)* laughs with his *NFL Sunday* cohosts Howie Long *(left)* and James Brown *(right)* during a visit to the USS *Harry S. Truman* on December 14, 2000.

Bradshaw's New Team

Despite the rocky start to his announcing career, television executives and viewers alike enjoyed his relaxed and colorful style of announcing. He was a breath of fresh air in a profession that was typically straitlaced and serious. Bradshaw cracked jokes, sang songs, and had fun.

Today, he is a member of an Emmy Award–winning football show on the FOX network called *NFL Sunday*. Bradshaw and his "teammates" James Brown, Howie Long, and Cris Collinsworth have become a big hit for several reasons. They all certainly know a lot about football, but mostly they just like to enjoy themselves. *NFL Sunday* is the perfect place for Bradshaw to show off his original style and hilarious personality while doing what he loves best of all: talking about football.

6 Terry Bradshaw and the Hall of Fame

The Pro Football Hall of Fame, located in Canton, Ohio, officially opened on September 7, 1963. That day, 17 legendary football players were inducted, including Olympic great Jim Thorpe.

Terry Bradshaw was inducted into the Hall of Fame in 1989, the first year he was eligible (a player has to be retired for five years before he can be eligible). All his life, Bradshaw had dreamed about playing with the pros and winning Super Bowls. He also dreamed about making it to the Hall of Fame, a goal very few players achieve. It is considered the ultimate award. Bradshaw was overjoyed to receive this honor. "I've always downplayed awards," he later wrote in his book *Looking Deep*, "but this one would be

Terry Bradshaw poses with his bust after being inducted into the Pro Football Hall of Fame in 1989.

the last I would ever receive in football." This award meant a lot to Terry Bradshaw, as it does for most Hall of Famers.

Impressive Stats

A look at Bradshaw's achievements on the field reveals why he was selected to join the Hall of Fame. Bradshaw set a long list of significant records during his career (although many of them have since been broken): 9 Super Bowl touchdown passes and 932 yards passing; 30 playoff touchdown passes and 3,833 yards passing; and leading the same team to back-to-back Super Bowls twice. Over his entire career, Bradshaw passed for a total 27,989 yards. He threw 212 touchdown passes, ran 2,257 yards, and ran for 32 touchdowns. He was 1978 AFC Player of the Year, and he was named Super Bowl MVP for the 1978 and 1979 seasons. He was selected for the 1975, 1978, and 1979 AFC Pro Bowl teams. As of this book's publication, Bradshaw still holds most quarterback records for the Pittsburgh Steelers and all passing and total offense records for Louisiana Tech.

In the end, Terry Bradshaw, whom many considered too unintelligent to lead a team's offense when he began his pro career in 1970, became one of football's most impressive quarterbacks.

"Thank You, Pittsburgh"

Bradshaw gave a memorable acceptance speech when he was inducted into the Hall of Fame. Always the comedian, he made sure his audience had a good laugh. According to Bradshaw's Bullet (http://www.mcmillenandwife. com/bradshaw.html), Terry opened his speech with the following: "I can't find the words to thank [Hall of Fame Director] Pete Elliott enough. I know he's spent the fifty thousand I sent him to make sure I got in here." Bradshaw thanked many people, especially his teammates. He said he would not have been elected into the Hall of Fame without the people he played with. "Thank you number eighty-eight, Lynn Swann! Thank you number eighty-two, John Stallworth! Thank you, Franco Harris! Thank you, Rock Bleier! What I wouldn't give right now to put my hands under [center] Mike Webster's butt just one more time! Thank you, Mike!"

He also addressed his favorite style of play: going deep. "My nature was attack. Throw it deep. Anybody can throw wide, let's go deep!" The crowd, seemingly full of Pittsburgh Steelers fans, cheered his every word.

For a moment, Bradshaw looked like he was going to break down in tears of joy. Terry had always been fond of Pittsburgh Steelers owner Art Rooney, who had died the previous year in 1988. Terry looked into the sky and said, "Art Rooney, boy, I loved that man. I know you're watching, Art. I love you. You were always, always by me. I love you so much! Thank you. Pittsburgh, hey, I love you!"

Timeline

September 2, 1948 Terry Paxton Bradshaw is born in Shreveport, Louisiana.

1957 Bradshaw plays his first official football game.

1965 Bradshaw sets national high school javelin record, 244 feet, 11¾ inches.

1966 Bradshaw enrolls at Louisiana Tech University.

1969 Bradshaw leads his senior team to the NCAA College Division Mideast Championship game in the Grantland Rice Bowl—Bradshaw's first televised game. He impressed pro scouts, leading his team to a 33–13 victory over the Akron Zips.

1970 Bradshaw is taken first overall by the Pittsburgh Steelers in the NFL draft.

September 1970 Bradshaw plays his first pro game in the NFL against the Houston Oilers but is pulled out halfway through the game. The Pittsburgh Steelers lose 7–19.

December 23, 1972 The Pittsburgh Steelers beat the Oakland Raiders to win their first playoff game ever by a score of 13–7. Bradshaw completes the game-winning pass to Franco Harris in the last seconds of the game. This pass, known as the Immaculate Reception, goes down in NFL history as the most amazing and most contested play ever.

January 12, 1975 Super Bowl IX, New Orleans, Louisiana. The Pittsburgh Steelers beat the Minnesota Vikings

16–6. This is the first of four Super Bowl wins for the Pittsburgh Steelers led by Bradshaw as quarterback.

January 18, 1976 Super Bowl X, Miami, Florida. The Pittsburgh Steelers beat the Dallas Cowboys 21–17. Bradshaw is knocked unconscious after throwing the game-winning pass.

1976 Bradshaw selected to play in the Pro Bowl but is unable to play due to an injury.

January 21, 1979 Super Bowl XIII, Miami, Florida. The Pittsburgh Steelers beat the Dallas Cowboys 35–31. Bradshaw is unanimously elected MVP. He throws for 318 yards and four touchdowns, setting a Super Bowl record.

1979 Bradshaw plays in the Pro Bowl for the AFC.

January 20, 1980 Super Bowl XIV, Pasadena, California. The Pittsburgh Steelers beat the Los Angeles Rams 31–19. Bradshaw wins his second consecutive MVP award.

1980 Bradshaw plays in the Pro Bowl for the AFC.

1982 Bradshaw injures his throwing arm early in the season. This proves to be a career-ending injury.

1983 Bradshaw plays the last game of his career. His final play is a touchdown pass.

1984 Bradshaw officially retires after 14 years with the Pittsburgh Steelers.

1984 Bradshaw becomes a television announcer for CBS.

1989 Bradshaw is inducted into the Football Hall of Fame the first year he is eligible.

1996 Bradshaw joins *NFL Sunday* on FOX Television.

Glossary

all-pro teams Two teams made up of the best players from the AFC and the NFC that play an exhibition game each year after the season is over.

blitz A play in which defensive players rush at the quarterback instead of covering their normal positions.

down A single play during a football game. The offense has four downs to move the ball forward ten yards or score.

dynasty A pro sports team that wins several championship games in a short period of time.

end zone The area behind each goal line on a football field. A team must reach the other team's end zone with the football to score a touchdown.

fumble A play in which a player on the offense drops the football. Any player may recover the ball after a fumble.

gridiron A football field.

huddle A circle formed by the offensive players in the time between each down in which they plan the next play.

interception A play in which a pass is caught by a defensive player instead of the intended offensive player.

playoffs The postseason tournament that results in the Super Bowl. The top 12 teams make it to the playoffs.

rookie A player in his or her first year on a team.

sack To tackle the quarterback before he can throw the ball.

scout A person who travels around the country looking for talented new players for sports teams.

scramble A maneuver in which the quarterback moves around quickly while looking for a receiver to throw to.

sideline The very edge of the football field and the area behind it where players stand when they are not playing.

Super Bowl A game played once a year between the AFC champion and the NFC champion to decide the champion of the NFL.

touchdown A touchdown is scored when an offensive player either crosses the goal line with the football or makes a reception inside the end zone; it is worth six points.

For More Information

Louisiana Tech University
P.O. Box 3178
Ruston, LA 71272
(318) 257-3036
Web site: http://www.latech.edu

National Attention Deficit Disorder Association
1788 Second Street, Suite 200
Highland Park, IL 60035
(847) 432-ADDA
Web site: http://www.add.org

The National Collegiate Athletic Association
700 West Washington Street
P.O. Box 6222
Indianapolis, IN 46206-6222
(317) 917-6222

The National Football League, Inc.
280 Park Avenue
New York, NY 10017
(212) 450-2000
Web site: http://www.nfl.com

Pittsburgh Steelers
Administrative Offices
3400 South Water Street
Pittsburgh, PA 15203-2349
(412) 432-7800

Pittsburgh Steelers
Ticket Office
1501 Reedsdale Street, Suite 204
Pittsburgh, PA 15233
(412) 432-7800

Pro Football Hall of Fame
2121 George Halas Drive NW
Canton, OH 44708
(330) 456-8207
Web site: http://www.profootballhof.com

Web Sites

Due to the changing nature of Internet links, the Rosen Publishing Group, Inc., has developed an online list of Web sites related to the subject of this book. This site is updated regularly. Please use this link to access the list:

http://www.rosenlinks.com/fhf/tbra/

For Further Reading

Bradshaw, Terry, and David Diles. *Man of Steel*. Grand Rapids, MI: Zondervan, 1980.

Bradshaw, Terry, and David Fisher. *It's Only a Game*. New York: Pocket Books, 2001.

Bradshaw, Terry, and Buddy Martin. *Looking Deep*. New York: Berkley, 1991.

Buckley, James, Jr. *Eyewitness: Football*. New York: Dorling Kindersley, 1999.

Buckley, James, Jr. *Eyewitness: Super Bowl*. New York: Dorling Kindersley, 2000.

Christopher, Matt. *Great Moments in Football History*. Boston: Little, Brown & Co., 1997.

Fitzgerald, Francis J. *Greatest Moments in Pittsburgh Steelers History*. Bedford, KY: AdCraft, 1996.

Long, Howie. *Football for Dummies*. Los Angeles, CA: Hungry Minds, 1998.

Mendelson, Abby. *Pittsburgh Steelers: the Official Team History.* Dallas, TX: Taylor Publishing, 1996.

Prentzas, G. S. *Terry Bradshaw.* Broomall, PA: Chelsea House, 1994.

Silverstein, Herma, and Terry J. Dunnahoo. *Pro Football Hall of Fame.* Parsippany, NJ: Silver Burdett Press, 1994.

Time-Life Editors. *Sports Illustrated: Best Super Bowls.* Alexandria, VA: Time-Life, Inc., 1998.

Bibliography

Bradshaw, Terry, and David Diles. *Man of Steel*. Grand Rapids, MI: Zondervan, 1980.

Bradshaw, Terry, and David Fisher. *It's Only a Game*. New York: Pocket Books, 2001.

Bradshaw, Terry, and Buddy Martin. *Looking Deep*. New York: Berkley, 1991.

Play Football: The Official NFL Site for Kids. Retrieved January 6, 2002 (http://www. playfootball.com).

Pro Football Hall of Fame. Retrieved January 6, 2002 (http://www.profootballhof.com).

SportingNews.com. Retrieved January 6, 2002 (http://tsn.sportingnews.com/archives/ superbowl.html).

Index

Index

About the Author

Greg Roza writes and edits for a children's book publisher located in western New York. In his spare time, he teaches poetry at SUNY Fredonia. Greg and his wife, Abigail, have a daughter named Autumn.

Photo Credits

Cover, pp. 4, 10–11, 17, 38, 57, 62, 79 © Bettmann/Corbis; p. 27 courtesy of Louisiana Tech Athletic Media Relations; p. 33 © Philip Good/Corbis; pp. 36–37, 52–53, 61, 65, 68–69, 74–75, 77, 87, 90–91, 94 © AP/Wide World Photos; pp. 44–45, 82, 88 © Sports Chrome; pp. 48, 96 © Chock Solomin/Icon SMI.

Design and Layout

Tahara Hasan